333

Wittiest
Quotable
Quotes

Jakub Marian

First Edition, April 2014

ISBN-13: 978-1499199109

Printed by: On-Demand Publishing LLC, 100 Enterprise Way, Suite A200, Scotts Valley, CA 95066, USA

Author and Publisher: Jakub Marian, Sewanstraße 217, 10319, Berlin, Germany

Before you start reading

You are reading the paperback version of this book. If you happen to have found this book freely available on the Internet (from an illegal source), please consider buying a legal copy (there is a PDF, Kindle, and Paperback edition) which is also the only one guaranteed to be up to date. You can find links to all the versions at

http://jakubmarian.com/witty-quotes/

If you bought this book, you are allowed to make as many (electronic or physical) copies as you wish and distribute them to all members of your household. You are not allowed to make the book available publicly; if you wish to send it to someone not within your household, simply buy another paper or electronic copy.

If you find any error in the book, please send an email with a description of the error to

errors@jakubmarian.com

Table of Contents

Foreword

People say that a picture is worth a thousand words, but sometimes a mighty quotation is worth more than a thousand pictures. Words have the ability to express thoughts, and also the power to make us laugh. It is when these two abilities are skilfully combined that a special kind of quotes that we so adore emerges.

This book contains a selection of 333 such quotations, carefully selected in a strict editorial process—they are mostly short, intelligent, funny, often sharp and sarcastic, and most importantly, quotable.

There are many books on the market, as well as freely accessible websites, that will allow you to find quotes related to a given subject. You'll find thousands or even tens of thousands of quotes there, but most of them are of mediocre quality and hardly any of them can be used in a conversation, in a speech, or in a written essay.

That's why I decided to fight my way through this jungle of quotes and compile the best of them in a book that can be read from cover to cover. I believe that dividing the quotes up in categories would make reading the book rather dull (I'd compare it to eating the main course and all the sides separately instead of in a delicious mix), so I decided not to do so. If you want to find a quote and you know approximately what the quote was about, it is generally easier to find it online using a search engine rather than trying to locate the source where you read the quote for the first time.

Also, great care has been put into finding the original author of each quote. If the original author of a quote remains in obscurity, he or she is listed as Anonymous. If a quote is attributed to an author by modern sources (even if contemporary sources are missing) the name written here accords with this modern attribution.

I wish you a pleasant reading experience and hope you will enjoy reading the book as much as I enjoyed writing it.

Jakub Marian
(the editor)

How to quote

Of course, you cannot just blurt out a quote whenever you feel like it. For a quote to have the desired effect, it must be properly introduced. One way of introducing a quote, especially if its author is unknown or not notable, is using the phrase "a wise man/woman once said".

If you happen to know the author's occupation and it is related to the quote's content, you can refer to them using their occupation, e.g. "a German philosopher once wrote" or "an American journalist once said". This is an especially useful tool when the author's nationality is to be emphasized.

When the author is notable enough, it's usually best to introduce the quotation using his or her name, e.g. "Mark Twain once said", "In the words of Mark Twain", "It was Mark Twain who said", "There's a beautiful quote by Mark Twain".

If you don't know the source of the quote you want to cite at the moment, it's usually best to admit it and introduce it by something like "there's a great quote on the topic, but I can't remember who said it". You can also try and misattribute it to enhance the credibility of the quote, as in the following example:

> *If you don't know the source of a quote, you can always make it sound better by attributing it to me.*
>
> — *Mark Twain*

Of course, Mark Twain never said that—the quote was made up by me to illustrate the power of misattribution. However, I **discourage** *consciously* misattributing quotes, as it is both unethical and you can alienate those who knew it was a misattribution.

Sometimes, however, an obvious misattribution can be used for a comic effect or to reinforce the message of the quote, as in:

> *Don't believe everything you read on the Internet.*
>
> — *Abraham Lincoln*

But don't worry; you will find no such misattributions in this book.

Quotes

I always have a quotation for everything—it saves original thinking.

— *Dorothy L. Sayers*

~

They laughed when I said I was going to be a comedian... They are not laughing now.

— *Bob Monkhouse*

~

Illegal aliens have always been a problem in the United States. Ask any Indian.

— *Robert Orben*

He had a mind so fine no idea could violate it.

— *T. S. Eliot*

~

I've had a perfectly wonderful evening, but this wasn't it.

— *Groucho Marx*

~

If you're too open-minded, your brains will fall out.

— *Lawrence Ferlinghetti*

~

Somebody actually complimented me on my driving today. They left a little note on the windscreen. It said: 'Parking fine'.

— *Tommy Cooper*

Giving up smoking is the easiest thing in the world. I know because I've done it thousands of times.

— Mark Twain

California is a fine place to live—if you happen to be an orange.

— *Fred Allen*

~

Sex without love is a meaningless experience, but as far as meaningless experiences go, it's pretty damn good.

— *Woody Allen*

~

If governments are involved in covering up the knowledge of aliens then they are doing a much better job of it than they seem to do at anything else.

— *Stephen Hawking*

~

Atheism is a non-prophet organization.

— *George Carlin*

I always keep a supply of stimulant handy in case I see a snake—which I also keep handy.

— W. C. Fields

~

Writing about music is like dancing about architecture.

— Anonymous

~

'Do you pray for the senators, Dr. Hale?'
'No, I look at the senators and pray for the country.'

— Edward Everett Hale
(American Unitarian clergyman)

~

A bargain is something you don't need at a price you can't resist.

— Franklin Jones

Last year I gave several lectures on 'Intelligence and the Appreciation of Music Among Animals'. Today I am going to speak to you about 'Intelligence and the Appreciation of Music Among Critics'. The subject is very similar.

— *Erik Satie*

~

I once heard a Californian student in Heidelberg say, in one of his calmest moods, that he would rather decline two drinks than one German adjective.

— *Mark Twain*

~

Don't go around saying the world owes you a living. The world owes you nothing. It was here first.

— *Mark Twain*

I refuse to think of them as chin hairs. I think of them as stray eyebrows.

— Janette Barber

~

In England, justice is open to all—like the Ritz Hotel.

*— James Mathew
(Irish Judge)*

~

You know everybody is ignorant, only on different subjects.

— Will Rogers

~

The length of a film should be directly related to the endurance of the human bladder.

— Alfred Hitchcock

Whenever you find yourself on the side of the majority, it is time to pause and reflect.

— *Mark Twain*

~

A dress has no meaning unless it makes a man want to take it off.

— *Françoise Sagan*

~

Is Moby Dick the whale or the man?

— *Harold Ross*

~

The most beautiful words in the English language are not 'I love you' but 'It's benign'.

— *Woody Allen*

If we knew what it was we were doing, it would not be called research, would it?

— Albert Einstein

I have noticed that the people who are late are often so much jollier than the people who have to wait for them.

— *E. V. Lucas*

∾

If I were two-faced, would I be wearing this one?

— *Abraham Lincoln*

∾

My dad was the town drunk. Usually that's not so bad, but New York City?

— *Henny Youngman*

∾

The difference between life and the movies is that a script has to make sense, and life doesn't.

— *Joseph L. Mankiewicz*

Knowledge is knowing a tomato is a fruit; wisdom is not putting it in a fruit salad.

> — *Miles Kington*

~

If only God would give me some clear sign! Like making a large deposit in my name at a Swiss Bank.

> — *Woody Allen*

~

By an unnamed professor at Ohio University: I am returning this otherwise good typing paper to you because someone has printed gibberish all over it and put your name at the top.

> — *Quoted in New Scientist, 1996*

Millions saw the apple fall, but Newton was the one who asked why.

> — *Bernard M. Baruch*

Being powerful is like being a lady. If you have to tell people you are, you aren't.

> — *Margaret Thatcher*

The most difficult thing in the world is to know how to do a thing and to watch someone else do it wrong without comment.

> — *T. H. White*

Happiness is good health and a bad memory.

> — *Ingrid Bergman*

Never criticize Americans. They have the best taste that money can buy.

— *Miles Kington*

See, the problem is that God gives men a brain and a penis, and only enough blood to run one at a time.

— *Robin Williams*

Right now I'm having amnesia and déja vu at the same time. I think I've forgotten this before.

— *Steven Wright*

To err is human—but it feels divine.

— *Mae West*

The depressing thing about tennis is that no matter how good I get, I'll never be as good as a wall.

— *Mitch Hedberg*

~

Of a dinner for Nobel Prize laureates at the White House: Probably the greatest concentration of talent and genius in this house except perhaps those times when Thomas Jefferson ate alone.

— *John F. Kennedy*

~

The Norwegian language has been described as German spoken underwater.

— *Anonymous*

~

When we talk to God, we're praying. When God talks to us, we're schizophrenic.

— *Jane Wagner*

Ladies, if a man says he will fix it, he will. There's no need to remind him every six months about it.

— *Anonymous*

∾

Wife: Cooking! Cleaning! Why should women do it?
Husband: You're quite right—let's get an au pair girl.

— *Mel Calman*

∾

Don't talk unless you can improve the silence.

— *Jorge Luis Borges*

∾

When asked what he would like to see on his tombstone: Keep off the grass.

— *Peter Ustinov*

It's not that I'm afraid to die, I just don't want to be there when it happens.

— *Woody Allen*

~

The photograph is not quite true to my own notion of my gentleness and sweetness of nature, but neither perhaps is my external appearance.

— *A. E. Housman*

~

The only reason some people get lost in thought is because it's unfamiliar territory.

— *Paul Fix*

~

'My idea of an agreeable person,' said Hugo Bohun, 'is a person who agrees with me.'

— *Benjamin Disraeli*

My inclination to go by the Air Express is confirmed by the crash they had yesterday, which will make them more careful in the immediate future.

— A. E. Housman

~

Insanity is hereditary. You get it from your children.

— Sam Levenson

~

I go to the theatre to be entertained, I want to be taken out of myself, I don't want to see lust and rape and incest and sodomy and so on, I can get all that at home.

— Alan Bennett

~

You can learn many things from children. How much patience you have, for instance.

— Franklin P. Adams

After a while, marriage is a sibling relationship—marked by occasional, and rather regrettable, episodes of incest.

— *Martin Amis*

~

There was laughter in the back of the theatre, leading to the belief that someone was telling jokes back there.

— *George S. Kaufman*
(American playwright)

~

I think the worst time to have a heart attack is during a game of charades.

— *Demetri Martin*

~

If you can't be a good example, then you'll just have to be a horrible warning.

— *Catherine Aird*

At the age of six I wanted to be a cook. At seven I wanted to be Napoleon. And my ambition has been growing steadily ever since.

— *Salvador Dali*

≈

The only person entitled to use the imperial 'we' in speaking of himself is a king, an editor, and a man with a tapeworm.

— *Robert G. Ingersoll*

≈

I like work; it fascinates me. I can sit and look at it for hours.

— *Jerome K. Jerome*

≈

In 1969 I gave up women and alcohol. It was the worst 20 minutes of my life.

— *George Best*

I'm tired of all this nonsense about beauty
being only skin-deep. That's deep enough.
What do you want—an adorable pancreas?

— *Jean Kerr*

～

Nostalgia isn't what it used to be.

— *Anonymous*

～

Opera is when a guy gets stabbed in the back
and, instead of bleeding, he sings.

— *Ed Gardner*

～

Millions long for immortality who don't
know what to do with themselves on a rainy
Sunday afternoon.

— *Susan Ertz*

Whoever said 'it's not whether you win or lose that counts' probably lost.

> — *Martina Navrátilová*

~

I intend to live forever. So far, so good.

> — *Steven Wright*

~

Do unto others before they do unto you.

> — *Anonymous*

~

There was the actor who put in his will that he wanted to be cremated and ten percent of his ashes thrown in his agent's face.

> — *Harry Richman*

All pro athletes are bilingual. They speak English and profanity.

— Gordie Howe

~

On the Atkins diet: You die of a heart attack but so what? You die thin.

— Bob Geldof

~

Why do born-again people so often make you wish they'd never been born the first time?

— Katharine Whitehorn

~

If you're not failing every now and again, it's a sign you're not doing anything very innovative.

— Woody Allen

You can get much farther with a kind word and a gun than you can with a kind word alone.

— Al Capone

A French chef's view: English cooking: put things in hot water and take them out again after a while.

— *Anonymous*

~

I'm on a whiskey diet. I've lost three days already.

— *Tommy Cooper*

~

It matters not whether you win or lose: what matters is whether I win or lose.

— *Darin Weinberg*

~

Under democracy one party always devotes its energies to trying to prove that the other party is unfit to rule—and both commonly succeed and are right.

— *H. L. Mencken*

The French, they say, live to eat. The
English, on the other hand, eat to die.

— *Martin Amis*

∽

I never forget a face, but in your case I'll be
glad to make an exception.

— *Groucho Marx*

∽

When I was a boy I was told that anybody
could become President. Now I'm beginning
to believe it.

— *Clarence Darrow*

∽

She's been kissed oftener than a police-court
Bible and by much the same class of people.

— *Robertson Davies*

I love children, especially when they cry, for then someone takes them away.

— *Nancy Mitford*

~

An economist is an expert who will know tomorrow why the things he predicted yesterday didn't happen today.

— *Laurence J. Peter*

~

A successful man is one who makes more money than his wife can spend. A successful woman is one who can find such a man.

— *Lana Turner*

~

Procrastination is the art of keeping up with yesterday.

— *Don Marquis*

Judge: Are you trying to show contempt for this court?
Mae West: No, I'm doing my best to hide it.

— *Mae West*

∽

The fewer the facts, the stronger the opinion.

— *Arnold H. Glasow*

∽

A man explained inflation to his wife thus: 'When we married you measured 36-24-36. Now you're 42-42-42. There's more of you, but you're not worth as much.'

— *Joel Barnett*

∽

I don't hate you... I just don't like that you exist.

— *Gena Showalter*

When asked whether he really believed horseshoe hanging over his door would bring him luck: Of course not, but I am told it works even if you don't believe in it.

— *Niels Bohr*

~

Many a man owes his success to his first wife and his second wife to his success.

— *Jim Backus*

~

When a girl marries, she exchanges the attentions of many men for the inattention of one.

— *Helen Rowland*

~

Should not the Society of Indexers be known as Indexers, Society of, The?

— *Keith Waterhouse*

Critics are like eunuchs in a harem; they know how it's done, they've seen it done every day, but they're unable to do it themselves.

— *Brendan Behan*

On the reunification of Germany: It's like the Beatles coming together again—let's hope they don't go on a world tour.

— *Matt Frei*

A woman's mind is cleaner than a man's; she changes it more often.

— *Oliver Herford*

Cats, I always think, only jump into your lap to check if you are cold enough, yet, to eat.

— *Anne Enright*

The best computer is a man, and it's the only one that can be mass-produced by unskilled labor.

— Wernher von Braun

~

I would challenge you to a battle of wits, but I see you are unarmed.

— William Shakespeare

~

Having children makes you no more a parent than having a piano makes you a pianist.

— Michael Levine

~

Of Arnold Schwarzenegger: I once described him as looking like a brown condom full of walnuts.

— Clive James

Wherever my dad is now, he's looking down on me... not because he's dead, but because he is very condescending.

— *Jack Whitehall*

~

Acting is merely the art of keeping a large group of people from coughing.

— *Ralph Richardson*

~

Middle age is when your broad mind and narrow waist begin to change places.

— *E. Joseph Cossman*

~

An archaeologist is the best husband a woman can have; the older she gets the more interested he is in her.

— *Agatha Christie*

There's one thing to be said for inviting trouble: it generally accepts.

— *Mae Maloo*

~

To find a friend one must close one eye. To keep him—two.

— *Norman Douglas*

~

'What are you painting?' I said. 'Is it the Heavenly Child?' 'No' he said, 'It is a cow.'

— *Stephen Leacock*

~

Change is inevitable—except from a vending machine.

— *Robert C. Gallagher*

Like all great travellers, I have seen more than I remember, and remember more than I have seen.

— *Benjamin Disraeli*

～

She never lets ideas interrupt the easy flow of her conversation.

— *Jean Webster*

～

I've never won an argument with her; and the only times I thought I had I found the argument wasn't over yet.

— *Jimmy Carter*

～

I can speak Esperanto like a native.

— *Spike Milligan*

God in His wisdom made the fly
And then forgot to tell us why.

> — *Ogden Nash*

~

Always be sincere, even if you don't mean it.

> — *Harry S. Truman*

~

Whenever I'm on my computer, I don't type
'lol'. I type 'lqtm': 'laugh quietly to myself'.
It's more honest.

> — *Demetri Martin*

~

It's not what you don't know that kills you,
it's what you know for sure that ain't true.

> — *Mark Twain*

My love life is terrible. The last time
I was inside a woman was when I
visited the Statue of Liberty.

— Woody Allen

I want a man who's kind and understanding.
Is that too much to ask of a millionaire?

— *Zsa Zsa Gabor*

Have you ever noticed that anybody driving
slower than you is an idiot, and anyone
going faster than you is a maniac?

— *George Carlin*

Clothes make the man. Naked people have
little or no influence on society.

— *Mark Twain*

First the doctor told me the good news: I
was going to have a disease named after me.

— *Steve Martin*

Blessed is the man who, having nothing to say, abstains from giving us a wordy evidence of the fact.

— *George Eliot*

~

I never travel without my diary. One should always have something sensational to read in the train.

— *Oscar Wilde*

~

A specialist is a man who knows more and more about less and less.

— *William Mayo*

~

Alcohol doesn't solve any problems... but then again, neither does milk.

— *Anonymous*

The important thing when you are going to do something brave is to have someone on hand to witness it.

— Michael Howard

∾

To write one's memoirs is to speak ill of everybody except oneself.

— Henri Philippe Pétain

∾

What they call 'heart' lies much lower than the fourth waistcoat button.

— Georg Christoph Lichtenberg

∾

England and America are two countries divided by a common language.

— George Bernard Shaw

My books are water; those of the great geniuses is wine. Everybody drinks water.

— *Mark Twain*

≈

I wouldn't say I was the best manager, but I was in the top one.

— *Brian Clough*

≈

I've lived through some terrible things in my life, some of which actually happened.

— *Mark Twain*

≈

God created war so that Americans would learn geography.

— *Mark Twain*

I won't say she was silly, but I think one of us was silly, and it wasn't me.

— *Elizabeth Gaskell*

≈

A man who correctly guesses a woman's age may be smart, but he's not very bright.

— *Lucille Ball*

≈

I would have answered your letter sooner, but you didn't send one.

— *Goodman Ace*

≈

You know that look women get when they want to have sex? Me neither.

— *Steve Martin*

There are no bad pictures; that's just how your face looks sometimes.

— Abraham Lincoln

In order for three people to keep a secret, two must be dead.

— *Benjamin Franklin*

~

Nothing is more responsible for the good old days than a bad memory.

— *Franklin P. Adams*

~

Restaurant critics—even great critics are like very bad lovers. They only come once a year, they don't care if you're not ready, they leave without saying a word and then they tell everyone what you did was wrong.

— *Trevor White*

~

Every one says forgiveness is a lovely idea, until they have something to forgive.

— *C. S. Lewis*

I used to believe that chiropractors were charlatans, but then I went to one and now I stand corrected.

— *Shmuel Breban*

～

You start playing rock 'n' roll so you can have sex and do drugs. But you end up doing drugs so you can still play rock 'n' roll and have sex.

— *Mick Jagger*

～

On receiving an invitation for 9 a.m.: Oh, are there two nine o'clocks in the day?

— *Tallulah Bankhead*

～

On dictionaries: Defining what is unknown in terms of something equally unknown.

— *Flann O'Brien*

Just when you've squared up to the solemn realization that life is a bitch, it turns round and does something nice just to confuse you.

— *Tom Holt*

~

Claire: How do you know you're... God?
Earl of Gurney: Simple. When I pray to Him I find I'm talking to myself.

— *Peter Barnes*

~

I don't think there's intelligent life on other planets. Why should other planets be any different from this one?

— *Bob Monkhouse*

~

I am free of all prejudice. I hate everyone equally.

— *W. C. Fields*

If my critics saw me walking over the Thames, they would say it was because I couldn't swim.

— Margaret Thatcher

Grandchildren don't make a man feel old; it's the knowledge that he's married to a grandmother.

— G. Norman Collie

Analyzing humor is like dissecting a frog. Few people are interested and the frog dies of it.

— E. B. White

If there is anybody here that I have forgotten to insult, I apologize.

— Johannes Brahms

He had the sort of face that makes you realise that God does have a sense of humour.

— *Bill Bryson*

∾

The only man I know who behaves sensibly is my tailor; he takes my measurements anew each time he sees me. The rest go on with their old measurements and expect me to fit them.

— *George Bernard Shaw*

∾

I think people should mate for life. Like pigeons, or Catholics.

— *Woody Allen*

∾

Work is the curse of the drinking classes.

— *Oscar Wilde*

The public have an insatiable curiosity to know everything, except what is worth knowing.

— *Oscar Wilde*

~

Growing old is mandatory, growing up is optional.

— *Elaine R. Davis*
(often misattributed to Bob
Monkhouse, Chili Davis,
or Barbara E. Johnson)

~

Man is one of the toughest of animated creatures. Only the anthrax bacillus can stand so unfavourable an environment for so long a time.

— *H. L. Mencken*

Last words before being killed by enemy fire:
They couldn't hit an elephant at this
distance...

— *John Sedgwick*
(American Union general)

~

I'm always ready to learn, although I do not
always like being taught.

— *Winston Churchill*

~

It should be a very happy marriage—they
are both so much in love with him.

— *Irene Thomas*

~

I have been told that Wagner's music is
better than it sounds.

— *Edgar Wilson 'Bill' Nye*

You are thirty-two. You are rapidly approaching the age when your body, whether it embarrasses you or not, begins to embarrass other people.

— *Alan Bennett*

❦

Science may be described as the art of systematic oversimplification.

— *Karl Popper*

❦

I ran into Isosceles. He has a great idea for a new triangle.

— *Woody Allen*

❦

Some cause happiness wherever they go; others, whenever they go.

— *Oscar Wilde*

The reason grandparents and grandchildren get along so well is that they have a common enemy.

— *Sam Levenson*

~

There was a young man called MacNabbiter
Who had an organ of prodigious diameter.
But it was not the size
That gave girls the surprise,
'Twas his rhythm—Iambic Pentameter.

— *Anonymous*

~

Please can we have no more complaints about the pauses in Tony Blair's speeches. They are the best parts.

— *David Guest*

The United States invariably does the right thing, after having exhausted every other alternative.

— Winston Churchill

Someone once asked me if my dream was to live on in the hearts of people, and I said I would prefer to live on in my apartment.

— *Woody Allen*

⌇

A bank is a place where they lend you an umbrella in fair weather and ask for it back when it begins to rain.

— *Robert Frost*

⌇

Someone told me that each equation I included in the book would halve the sales.

— *Stephen Hawking*

⌇

Whenever a copyright law is to be made or altered, then the idiots assemble.

— *Mark Twain*

Women who seek to be equal with men lack ambition.

— *Anonymous*
(sometimes wrongly attributed
to Marilyn Monroe)

∾

Our bombs are incredibly smart. In fact, our bombs are better educated than the average high school graduate. At least they can find Kuwait.

— *A. Whitney Brown*

∾

Wilde: I shall always regard you as the best critic of my plays.
Tree: But I have never criticized your plays.
Wilde: That's why.

— *Oscar Wilde*

I have the simplest tastes. I am always satisfied with the best.

— *Oscar Wilde*

~

Of Bible: A wonderful book, but there are some very queer things in it.

— *George V*
(British king)

~

The right to be heard does not automatically include the right to be taken seriously.

— *Hubert H. Humphrey*

~

When I die, I want to go peacefully like my grandfather did—in his sleep. Not yelling and screaming like the passengers in his car.

— *Bob Monkhouse*

Medals, they're like haemorrhoids. Sooner or later every asshole gets one.

— Billy Wilder

~

After it was pointed out that his fly-button was undone: No matter. The dead bird does not leave the nest.

— Winston Churchill

~

Behind every successful man you'll find a woman who has nothing to wear.

— Harold Coffin

~

My main problem is reconciling my gross habits with my net income.

— Errol Flynn

Science is interesting, and if you don't agree, you can fuck off.

— Richard Dawkins
(quoting an anonymous editor
of New Scientist Magazine)

~

He used to be fairly indecisive, but now he's not so certain.

— Peter Alliss

~

Genius is one percent inspiration, ninety-nine percent perspiration.

— Thomas Alva Edison

~

Science never solves a problem without creating ten more.

— George Bernard Shaw

Pollution: cirrhosis of the river.

— *Anonymous*

◦◦◦

Always remember that you are absolutely unique. Just like everyone else.

— *Margaret Mead*

◦◦◦

If bars don't serve drunk people, I don't think McDonald's should be able to serve fat people.

— *Anonymous*

◦◦◦

Although it is generally known, I think it's about time to announce that I was born at a very early age.

— *Groucho Marx*

It's true hard work never killed anybody, but I figure, why take the chance?

— *Ronald Reagan*

~

After you'd known Christine for any length of time, you found yourself fighting a desire to look into her ear to see if you could spot daylight coming the other way.

— *Terry Pratchett*

~

You can tell a lot about a woman by her hands. For instance, if they are placed around your throat, she's probably slightly upset...

— *Anonymous*

~

The covers of this book are too far apart.

— *Ambrose Bierce*

Consult, v. To seek another's approval of a course already decided on.

— *Ambrose Bierce*

~

In war it does not matter who is right, but who is left.

— *Gerald Ray Jordan*

~

'Classic' – a book which people praise and don't read.

— *Mark Twain*

~

Philosophy of science is about as useful to scientists as ornithology is to birds.

— *Richard P. Feynman*

Of her ex-husband: He would grab me in his arms, hold me close—and tell me how wonderful he was.

> — *Shelley Winters*

≈

An optimist is a girl who mistakes a bulge for a curve.

> — *Ring Lardner*

≈

We cherish our friends not for their ability to amuse us, but for ours to amuse them.

> — *Evelyn Waugh*

≈

Going to church doesn't make you a Christian any more than going to a garage makes you an automobile.

> — *Billy Sunday*

The play was a great success, but the audience was a total failure.

— Oscar Wilde

I'm not waiting until my hair turns white to become patient and wise. Nope, I'm dyeing my hair tonight.

— *Jarod Kintz*

~

To err is human; to forgive, infrequent.

— *Franklin P. Adams*

~

Marriage is the only war where one sleeps with the enemy.

— *Anonymous*

~

Never put off till tomorrow, what you can do the day after tomorrow.

— *Mark Twain*

We were so poor that if we woke up on Christmas day without an erection, we had nothing to play with.

— Frank McCourt

~

In examinations those who do not wish to know ask questions of those who cannot tell.

— Walter Raleigh

~

A lot of people are very critical of modern reproductive processes without understanding all the ins and outs.

— Robert Winston

~

Ballet: Men wearing pants so tight that you can tell what religion they are.

— Robin Williams

Asking a working writer what he thinks about critics is like asking a lamp-post how it feels about dogs.

— Christopher Hampton

~

If at first you don't succeed, then skydiving definitely isn't for you.

— Steven Wright

~

There even are places where English completely disappears. In America, they haven't used it for years!

— Alan Jay Lerner

~

A diplomat is someone who can tell you to go to hell in such a way that you will look forward to the trip.

— Caskie Stinnett

No intelligent idea can gain general acceptance unless some stupidity is mixed in with it.

— *Fernando Pessoa*

~

Politicians and diapers have one thing in common. They should both be changed regularly, and for the same reason.

— *José Maria de Eça de Queiroz*

~

I have never let my schooling interfere with my education.

— *Mark Twain*

~

Reality is something the human race doesn't handle very well.

— *Gore Vidal*

A team effort is a lot of people doing what I say.

— *Michael Winner*

~

Ever noticed that no matter what happens in one day, it exactly fits in the newspaper?

— *Jerry Seinfeld*

~

I support gay marriage because I believe they have a right to be just as miserable as the rest of us.

— *Kinky Friedman*

~

I am fond of pigs. Dogs look up to us. Cats look down on us. Pigs treat us as equal.

— *Winston Churchill*

During an examination at Oxford, Wilde was required to translate a passage from the Greek version of the New Testament. Having acquitted himself well, he was stopped, to which he replied: Oh, do let me go on, I want to see how it ends.

— *Oscar Wilde*

~

I think animal testing is a terrible idea; they get all nervous and give the wrong answers.

— *Anonymous*

~

It's a very sobering feeling to be up in space and realize that one's safety factor was determined by the lowest bidder on a government contract.

— *Alan Shepard*
(American astronaut)

I have nothing to declare except my genius.

— *Oscar Wilde*

The best thing about being married is
having someone who puts out the rubbish.

— *Ulrika Jonsson*

Happiness is having a large, loving, caring,
close-knit family in another city.

— *George Burns*

Puritanism. The haunting fear that
someone, somewhere, may be happy.

— *H. L. Mencken*

Enjoy life. There's plenty of time to be dead.

— Hans Christian Andersen

I always wanted to be somebody, but now I realise I should have been more specific.

— *Lily Tomlin*

≈

My favourite machine at the gym is the vending machine.

— *Caroline Rhea*

≈

Wise men speak because they have something to say; fools because they have to say something.

— *Plato*

≈

Of the US Senate: Office hours are from 12 to 1 with an hour off for lunch.

— *George S. Kaufman*

Life is pleasant. Death is peaceful. It's the transition that's troublesome.

— *Isaac Asimov*

~

Those who believe in telekinetics, raise my hand.

— *Kurt Vonnegut*

~

The young have aspirations that never come to pass, the old have reminiscences of what never happened.

— *Saki*

~

He's the kind of guy who would stop on his way down the aisle to get married to say hello to a pretty girl.

— *Tammy Wynette*

I told my wife the truth. I told her I was seeing a psychiatrist. Then she told me the truth: that she was seeing a psychiatrist, two plumbers, and a bartender.

— *Rodney Dangerfield*

Trickle-down theory—the less than elegant metaphor that if one feeds the horse enough oats, some will pass through to the road for the sparrows.

— *J. K. Galbraith*

Money is better than poverty, if only for financial reasons.

— *Woody Allen*

Yesterday is history. Tomorrow is a mystery. Today is a gift. That's why its called the present.

— *Alice Morse Earle*

~

When I left the dining room after sitting next to Mr Gladstone, I thought he was the cleverest man in England, but after sitting next to Mr Disraeli, I thought I was the cleverest woman in England.

— *Anonymous*
(sometimes attributed to Queen Victoria)

~

We've all heard that a million monkeys banging on a million typewriters will eventually reproduce the entire works of Shakespeare. Now, thanks to the Internet, we know this is not true.

— *Robert Wilensky*

Television is an invention that permits you to be entertained in your living room by people you wouldn't have in your home.

— *David Frost*

~

You know you are getting old when the candles cost more than the cake.

— *Bob Hope*

~

You can observe a lot just by watching.

— *Yogi Berra*

~

I did not attend his funeral, but I sent a nice letter saying approved of it.

— *Mark Twain*

The Lord prefers common-looking people.
That is why he made so many of them.

— Abraham Lincoln

~

To love oneself is the beginning of a lifelong
romance.

— Oscar Wilde

~

Some jokes are short and elegant, like a
mathematical proof or a midget in a ball-
gown.

— Demetri Martin

~

Early to rise and early to bed makes a male
healthy and wealthy and dead.

— James Thurber

The difference between Los Angeles and a yogurt is that yogurt has real culture.

— *Tom Taussik*

~

My love life is like a piece of Swiss cheese. Most of it's missing and what's there stinks.

— *Joan Rivers*

~

'For what we are about to receive,
Oh Lord, 'tis Thee we thank,'
Said the cannibal as he cut a slice
Of the missionary's shank.

— *E. Y. Harburg*

~

I believe in reincarnation, so I've left all my money to myself.

— *Tony Blackburn*

Politicians are the same all over. They promise to build a bridge even where there is no river.

— *Nikita Khrushchev*

~

One must have a heart of stone to read the death of little Nell without laughing.

— *Oscar Wilde*

~

Older people shouldn't eat health food, they need all the preservatives they can get.

— *Robert Orben*

~

Being published by the Oxford University Press is rather like being married to a duchess: the honour is almost greater than the pleasure.

— *G. M. Young*

There is nothing so annoying as to have two people go right on talking when you're interrupting.

— *Mark Twain*

~

Militant feminists, I take my hat off to them. They don't like that.

— *Milton Jones*

~

Kissinger brought peace to Vietnam the same way Napoleon brought peace to Europe: by losing.

— *Joseph Heller*

~

I distrust camels, and anyone else who can go a week without a drink.

— *Joe E. Lewis*

It's not true that I had nothing on. I had the radio on.

— Marilyn Monroe

Advertising may be described as the science of arresting human intelligence long enough to get money from it.

— *Stephen Leacock*

∾

Blessed is the man, who having nothing to say, abstains from giving wordy evidence of the fact.

— *George Eliot*

∾

I can't listen to too much Wagner, ya know? I start to get the urge to conquer Poland.

— *Woody Allen*

∾

Only one thing, is impossible for God: To find any sense in any copyright law on the planet.

— *Mark Twain*

Politics is the art of looking for trouble,
finding it whether it exists or not, diagnosing
it incorrectly, and applying
the wrong remedy.

— Ernest Benn

~

My life is all math. I am trying to add to my
income, subtract from my weight, divide my
time, and avoid multiplying.

— Anonymous

~

If you could kick the person in the pants
responsible for most of your trouble, you
wouldn't sit for a month.

— Theodore Roosevelt

~

Avant-garde? That's French for bullshit.

— John Lennon

Those people who think they know everything are a great annoyance to those of us who do.

— Isaac Asimov

~

If you steal from one author, it's plagiarism; if you steal from many, it's research.

— Wilson Mizner

~

I asked God for a bike, but I know God doesn't work that way. So I stole a bike and asked for forgiveness.

— Emo Philips

~

On the choice of the colour for the Model T Ford:
Any colour—so long as it's black.

— Henry Ford

He'd make a lovely corpse.

— Charles Dickens

~

He's really turned his life around. He used to be depressed and miserable. Now he's miserable and depressed.

— David Frost

~

There is only one thing in the world worse than being talked about, and that is not being talked about.

— Oscar Wilde

~

The world is full of willing people, some willing to work, the rest willing to let them.

— Robert Frost

Man is the only animal that blushes. Or needs to.

— *Mark Twain*

~

It is better to remain silent at the risk of being thought a fool, than to talk and remove all doubt of it.

— *Maurice Switzer*

~

Two things are infinite: the universe and human stupidity; and I'm not sure about the universe.

— *Albert Einstein*

~

Live so that you wouldn't be ashamed to sell the family parrot to the town gossip.

— *Will Rogers*

The secret of successful managing is to keep the five guys who hate you away from the four guys who haven't made up their minds.

— Charles Dillon Casey Stengel

~

I'm sure the universe is full of intelligent life. It's just been too intelligent to come here.

— Arthur C. Clarke

~

Bigamy is having one husband too many. Monogamy is the same.

— Anonymous

~

Status quo, you know, that is Latin for 'the mess we're in'.

— Ronald Reagan

On being asked to renounce the Devil on his deathbed: This is no time for making new enemies.

— *Voltaire*

∽

Saving is a very fine thing. Especially when your parents have done it for you.

— *Winston Churchill*

∽

When asked by his barber how he would like his hair cut: In silence.

— *Archelaus*

∽

A Merry Christmas to all my friends except two.

— *W. C. Fields*

Age is a question of mind over matter. If you don't mind, it doesn't matter.

— *Mark Twain*

∾

Abstract art: a product of the untalented sold by the unprincipled to the utterly bewildered.

— *Al Capp*

∾

The quickest way of ending a war is to lose it.

— *George Orwell*

∾

I don't believe in astrology; I'm a Sagittarius and we're sceptical.

— *Arthur C. Clarke*

I thought *coq au vin* was love in a lorry.

— *Victoria Wood*

~

Time is what we want most, but what we use worst.

— *William Penn*

~

The scientific theory I like best is that the rings of Saturn are composed entirely of lost airline luggage.

— *Mark Russell*

~

I was so ugly when I was born, the doctor slapped my mother.

— *Henny Youngman*

On plastic surgery: My body is a temple, and my temple needs redecorating.

— *Joan Rivers*

~

I must have a prodigious quantity of mind; it takes me as much as a week, sometimes, to make it up.

— *Mark Twain*

~

You have Van Gogh's ear for music.

— *Billy Wilder*

~

Interviewer: You've been accused of vulgarity.
Mel Brooks: Bullshit!

— *Mel Brooks*

The greatest thing in life is to die young—
but delay it as long as possible.

— George Bernard Shaw

∾

Behind every great man is a woman rolling
her eyes.

— Jim Carrey (in Bruce Almighty)

∾

A cow and calf are cut in half
And placed in separate cases
To call it art, however smart
Casts doubt on art's whole basis.

— Anonymous

∾

An alcoholic: A man you don't like who
drinks as much as you do.

— Dylan Thomas

I don't want to achieve immortality through my work... I want to achieve it through not dying.

— *Woody Allen*

～

I never hated a man enough to give him diamonds back.

— *Zsa Zsa Gabor*

～

A horse is dangerous at both ends and uncomfortable in the middle.

— *Ian Fleming*

～

I always invest in companies an idiot could run, because one day one will.

— *Warren Buffett*

I nearly missed the show tonight. I got to the Underground and saw this sign: 'Dogs must be carried on the escalators.' Took me forty minutes to find one.

— Harry Worth

～

A woman's dress should be like a barbed-wire fence: serving its purpose without obstructing the view.

— Sophia Loren

～

An Apology for the Devil: It must be remembered that we have only heard one side of the case. God has written all the books.

— Samuel Butler

It takes less time to do a thing right, than it does to explain why you did it wrong.

— *Henry Wadsworth Longfellow*

King David and King Solomon
Led merry, merry lives,
With many, many lady friends,
And many, many wives;
But when old age crept over them—
With many, many qualms!—
King Solomon wrote the Proverbs
And King David wrote the Psalms.

— *James Ball Naylor*

Final remarks

Thank you for your interest in my book; I hope you enjoyed reading it. You can read my articles and find my other books at

http://jakubmarian.com

You can follow me on

Google+: http://gplus.to/JakubMarian

Facebook: http://www.facebook.com/ JakubMarianOfficial

Mailing list: http://jakubmarian.com/ mailing-list/

If you find any error in the book, please send me an email with a description of the error to

errors@jakubmarian.com

Alphabetical Index